WHAT IF

68 QUESTIONS THAT WILL SHATTER YOUR PERCEPTION AND EXPAND THE WAY YOU LIVE LIFE

Corey Gladwell

INTRODUCTION

Crumpled, torn down, and destroyed overnight. I had lost every- thing. I was jobless, carless, penniless, and nearly homeless. Why was I lying here feeling like shit?

They say your early twenties are supposed to be the best years of your life. It is widely accepted that you take risks and are bold in this time of your life, because you have little commitments. I did everything I was meant to do, took risks, started companies, and made 'the money'. I had built up my empire from scratch: my nightclub, my restaurant, and my vodka brand. It was all something I used to think was a total success.

Yet here I was – a shell of the man I knew I could be, hollow and exhausted. There was nothing left in my life that seemed to matter anymore. Like a rubber band stretched too thin, I was dangerously close to snapping and breaking beyond any chance of restoration.

The chains had fallen off. I lost any drive that I may have once had. Material wealth was all that existed in my life and when that was not enough, I had nothing.

How did I let this happen? Why was my world disintegrating around me?

Suffering gave me every inspiration I needed to start my businesses and make money in the beginning.

From a destitute, public-benefit-dependent family, I quickly learnt that owning my own business was a way out of the poor life- style I was raised in. This kid-from-welfare mindset early infused in me, the tendency to be solely hyper-focused on money as the only means to success. And I did it. I made it out of poverty – and much more. I learnt many valuable lessons along the way. A major piece of wisdom I picked up was that the more you know, the more you can make. Knowledge is power. If you know how to run and operate a business, then you can be in charge of the business instead of it being in charge of you. If you know information, then you can sell information. If you know how to create a product, you can sell that product.

I spent a lot of time learning everything I could about business, life, anything I could get my hands on. I read book after book. I absorbed as much knowledge and information as I could, and then I implemented everything I learnt. I was in a position of power and eventually, I was able to share that knowledge with others.

I grew an empire; and then abruptly, I watched it fall. For a time, the businesses seemed to be going great. I was seeing the right metrics and hitting all my targets. Yet, instead of feeling joy and excitement in all these wins, my energy was constantly depleted. The desire to continue the daily grind and implement all the necessary systems to make sure my businesses were running smoothly faded away; no matter how hard I tried, my motivation was gone and the void in my soul could not be filled.

I had learnt so much, but there I was, January 2012, lying in my bed, sadly reflecting. I had everything – more cars, girls, money, friendships, and material success than I thought anyone could ever want; yet I was utterly lost and unsatisfied. At this point, I had given up, sold, or lost everything I had. I was barely more than homeless.

I had been in this state of despair and desolation for months before I started to realize that it was in fact my own set of beliefs and attitude towards making money to blame. The fact that I thought nothing else mattered, as well as my own experience of not feeling fulfilled internally, was the root of my empire's demise.

Then, I asked myself a question that changed it all. It was this: "Am I the only one in the world, the only one in the universe?" It was in that moment my mind snapped. There was a lesson I had not yet learnt. I realized it was just me, but not 'Corey Gladwell' me. Me as in this one being – the universe, experiencing itself as itself. I was the universe's eyes to see, its ears to hear, and I was here to fulfil its own desire.

All at once, my heart cracked open, allowing me to feel this unconditional love for everything and everyone on this planet. I was one with the bed, one with the walls, one with every person I met. I spent three weeks in this state of unconditional love, this total bliss and oneness with everything.

From emptiness, isolation, and total depression to this sur- real bliss, I finally saw that there was no such thing as separation. There was no such thing as duality, and in reality, all was one. That was what really changed my life trajectory. I stopped concentrating on that one golden prize: money. Instead, I wanted to give back to the world because I knew the world was myself.

When I realized that the world is truly a reflection of me, and that everything is me, I changed my focus of business, and how I was going to live my life. Business would now not be separate from spirituality; as my life would not be separate from my work. If I were ever going to get into business again, it would be to add value to other people's lives. I would come from a place of meaning and purpose. I would give people a transformation and fulfil them, because to fulfil them would be to fulfil myself.

This realization set me on a path. I now deeply understood that the longer you do not live out what you are truly here in this world to do, the more unsatisfied, empty and less fulfilled you be- come. This is important to comprehend. Not only can this dam- age your mental and emotional wellbeing but your physical health too. Your body will give you signs. It will get sick. It will develop problems. Not living true to yourself destroys your life and fills   it with catastrophes. This is the universe's way of nudging you   in the right direction, telling you to wake up and follow your true calling.

If you wake up every morning dreading going to a job you hate - one that you do just to pay the bills - your life will be unfulfilling and unsatisfying. There will always be a hint of emptiness in the back of your mind, knowing there is something else you are supposed to be doing. That's the very least. It can easily - and often does - go as far as sickness or divorce, or waking up at the age of 65 with a deep regret. I feel lucky that I was able to hit that moment of regret at 25 because I realized that the financial security, or the safety of working for someone else, was not quite enough.

You can see what is emerging in place of the more traditional view of 'get a job, have security, get a pay check' with this next generation. You can see the dissatisfaction with the older generations. You see the itch with younger generations; people want real life changing results. People want real experiences. The old way of entrepreneurship was to 'create a product and sell it'. Now, many people are in a search for meaning. Not just entrepreneurs, but the customers themselves. Customers want to know why you're doing what you are doing and what your motive is. Entrepreneurs want purpose in their mission, adding meaning to their service or product and how they serve their customers. You want fulfilment. Even if you make money, you make a product, or you have job, you still want meaning in your life.

That search for meaning is everywhere, and it causes a deep dissatisfaction, because where you are is not where you want to be. There is an everlasting sense of following your passion and your purpose, and bringing it into business. You want to be able to take risks and really get a reward out of it.

However, if you are one of those people who follow their passion and purpose, and bring it into business, the rewards are end- less. True fulfilment. Real joy. You will wake up extra early – two hours before you have to – and you will be excited to start what you used to call work; but now it no longer feels like work. You feel like your life is harmonious. You do not feel a separation between what you are supposed to do and what you want to do.

Those things all merge: your work, your family, your business. Everything becomes one thing, and you can truly have that complete wholeness that we all long for.

In the course of this book, I will insert summaries and action steps at the end of each chapter for you to take the knowledge you are gaining and make it a reality. I will make reference to important exercises in the bonus chapter at the end of this book. Information without action is meaningless. Hence, what I truly want for each individual I connect with is for him or her to change, to grow, to evolve, and to enlighten themselves.

My mission in life is to leave every person I meet – whether personally or through my work – better off than when I found them. That is my goal with this book. That is my goal with every- thing I do. My wish is for you to find your purpose, find your mission, carry a message, and deliver a transformation to those you meet. In life and in business, I imagine a world full of enlightened entrepreneurs living with purpose. A world full of people spreading a message of love and peace, producing transformations in their clients and friends, and living in enlightenment in action.

HOW TO USE THIS BOOK: ASK YOUR SELF

⌒﹏⌒

True growth comes from moments of self-realization. These peak experiences shatter the confines of our minds and extend us further than our perception previously allowed. By peak experiences, I mean "aha" moments that wake us up, whether profoundly or in small increments. My hope and intent for this book is that it will help you to move forward on your personal path and to experience more of these occasions of awakening, realization, and enlightenment.

To encourage and trigger more of these moments, all chapters provide short, easy-to-read contemplations, each followed by a question to ask yourself. Every contemplation is intended to provoke thought, to frame a thought process for its accompanying question.

Although some paths encourage adherents to empty them- selves of all thought, I believe we must go through our own search for understanding before we can move into an empty mind. Rather than fill you up with information you will quickly forget, the contemplations may stimulate your mind into following your own path.

After reading a contemplation, please take the time to ask yourself its corresponding question. You may wish to write down the answers that come. Each integration of a unique answer will lead you closer to a moment of self-actualization. Just be sure you are making up your own mind in the end. Only self-realization can lead to self-actualization, so you must answer these questions for yourself.

Again, this book is not meant to give you anyone else's pre- determined answers; instead, it can guide you to ask the right questions. You have your own answers. Deep down inside you is where all the right information is stored. I simply want to open the door so you may take a journey inside yourself. So find out what each concept means to you, then awaken to what you already know is true. My hope is that you take what you will from these pages and find your own realizations.

CHAPTER ONE

What If The Only Way To Get What You Want Is By Giving It To Others?

What if the secret to getting all your heart's desires lies in the act of giving them away? Maybe, just maybe, giving what you desire away freely to someone else will open something in you to receive it. If you want love? Give love. If you want money? Spend yours on someone in need. If you want gratitude? Help someone less fortunate. If you want to be appreciated? Sincerely tell someone how much you appreciate them.

I've heard it said before that "life supports that which sup- ports life". If you go out and give what it is you want, you'll get it in return. If you want help? Then find a way to be of help. Once you do, a shift will happen. Once you become a giver of what it is you are seeking, you will be filled with it. When we come from a place of lack, of desiring something we don't feel we have, we are telling the universe we are not enough. In turn, the universe will bring not enough back to us. But when we give that which we seek, we are in turn telling the universe we have more than enough. When that happens, the universe will bring to us more than enough. If we feel full, we shall stay full. Give and you shall receive

Ask Yourself: What If The Only Way To Get What You Want Is By Giving It To Others?

_____

_____

_____

_____

_____

_____

_____

_____

CHAPTER TWO

What If You Didn't Care About That Thing You Care About?

Just for a moment, let's step away from your life, at least mentally and emotionally. Take a step away and objectify your life, yourself, family, and friends. Take all ideas or concepts, all emotions and feelings, out of the equation, just for a few moments. Now take that one thing that just keeps getting on your nerves and bring it forward. Whether it's someone's behavior, words, or actions, whether it's the kids or spouse, parents or coworkers, friends or acquaintances, just bring that annoyance, frustration, or anger forward. Now imagine you suddenly don't care about it anymore. Imagine you not only don't care about it, but it doesn't phase you at all. How much better would your days go? How much more joy would you feel? How much less stress would you have? It may be hard, but just try to imagine that, in this moment, you just don't care about it anymore.

You cannot change anyone else. No matter how angry you get, how much you yell, how distant you become, you can't change them. You only have power over yourself, your thoughts, and your emotions. These are yours and you can change them. The truth is you don't have to care anymore. You don't have to get mad, frustrated, annoyed, or pissed off. You have the power to change that. That is in your control. This doesn't mean you have to stay at that job or with that person; but if you're going to make that choice, then accept the situation for what it is. No one will ever act exactly how you want them to act all the time. No one is perfect, not even you. People will say things and do things that won't fit your idea of who you want them to be, so it is up to you to decide what to care about.

How would you feel if you didn't believe they were wrong? How would you feel if you didn't care? Think about yourself and what negativity is doing to you? Think about how much better you would feel if you just let go?

Ask Yourself: What If You Didn't Care About That Thing You Care About?

_____

_____

_____

_____

_____

_____

_____

_____

CHAPTER THREE

What If You Accepted Everything In Your Life As Perfect?

Your life is perfect. How would it feel to believe that statement? How much gratitude would you feel if that statement was about your life? Why can't it be? I'm sure there's a long list of reasons a judgmental mind can conjure up. There's this, that, my job, my relationship, my family. On and on it goes as our egoic mind finds ways to justify our lack. But what if we could fully, completely accept our lives as perfect?

What if the job we have is a perfect learning tool to prepare us for our next one? If not having a job has given us the time to do the self-work necessary for our future happiness? If our relation- ship is our greatest teacher of tolerance and acceptance? If it's our perfect creation for us to finally know what love is and is not? If our children are our greatest teachers for how to live in the moment? If it is through them that we finally get to learn patience and unconditional love? What if your life is perfect, right here, right now? What if your life is exactly what you need in this moment for your greatest good?

Ask Yourself: What If You Accepted Everything In Your Life As Perfect?

_____

_____

_____

_____

_____

_____

_____

_____

CHAPTER FOUR

∿

What If Losing Your Job Was Exactly What You Needed?

Everyone has a deep desire, a longing for purpose, a passion to be fulfilled. If your job wasn't giving you at least a sense of purpose, then why carry on? Why regret losing a job if it wasn't fulfilling? Give yourself a dose of the truth. Be honest with what you want and go after it. Now is the time. Take every lesson you can from that previous employment and move on to what your heart and mind and wallet can all agree on. What they all want. What have you always dreamed of doing? What did you want to learn in school but never did? Now is the time. Take the chance and get on with it. Get on with the living part of life. Dive into the unknown with your heart set on your vision and watch how the universe takes care of the rest.

Ask Yourself: What If Losing Your Job Was Exactly What You Needed?

_____

_____

_____

_____

_____

_____

_____

CHAPTER FIVE

What If You Went Broke And That Was Your Freedom?

Going broke. Two words no one wants to say or even hear. No one ever wants to go broke. But what if that is the key to your dreams? When I was 23, I bought a nightclub in down town Seattle, then a restaurant. Oh, and then I launched a vodka brand. All in a few months, mainly from gathering investors together, since I didn't have that kind of income myself. The vodka brand lasted a few months, the restaurant a few more, and the nightclub a few years.

By the end of my run of "success", I was on so many drugs I couldn't keep track anymore. I was full of anxiety from all the stress and no matter what I bought, who I slept with, or how many people I had around me, I was depressed. Eventually, I lost it all. That was when I found everything I'd ever wanted. When I finally let go, when I totally surrendered, because I had nothing left to hold on to. That is when I found what I had been searching for my whole life. Freedom. Oneness with all of life. Unconditional love for all of life. Complete peace. That is what I received from going broke.

Who is anyone to say what can happen to you? I can only speak from my experience. If it takes losing it all to experience it, I would gladly sign up again. As a result of going broke, I have found my calling. I have found my purpose. I can love more deeply, laugh harder, and let go with a little more ease. Who knows what may be in store for each one of us, but who's to say that going broke won't hold the key to your freedom?

Ask Yourself: What If You Went Broke And That Was Your Freedom?

_____

_____

_____

_____

_____

_____

_____

CHAPTER SIX

What If You Couldn't Lie About Anything?

Imagine that. Always being honest, always telling the truth. What kind of world would we live in if no one could ever lie? To some, that might be a frightening concept. To me, it sounds like total freedom. No more worrying about covering your tracks, no more lying to cover another lie, just totally honest about everything. It can be a hard pill to swallow, but try it for a day. Spend one full day being completely honest with everyone. Tell them about what you think and how you feel. It doesn't have to be mean, rude, or even blunt. Just calmly and genuinely tell everyone the truth if they ask. This doesn't mean you have to push it on others, but if they ask, then be honest. What a world we could live in! Wouldn't you want everyone in your life to be honest with you? Then be honest with them. Have conscious, truthful conversations and see just how deep and intimate your relationships can become.

Ask Yourself: What If You Couldn't Lie About Anything?

_____

_____

_____

_____

_____

_____

_____

_____

Chapter Seven

What If You Let Yourself Be Happy Without External Circumstances?

You want this thing so you can be happy. You want this person so you can be happy. You want to go there so you can be happy. If only the situation would happen like this, then you could be happy. How about you cut out the middleman and just be happy? Think about how your days would go if you didn't need anything to happen to create happiness inside you. Just let it sink in. What if nothing needed to change, be done, created, or destroyed in order for you to have happiness? It's possible, and it's real. It's in your power to create your own happiness.

You have given people, places, and things the power to con- trol your happiness. All you have to do is take that power back. Nothing has the power to make you happy unless you let it. Likewise, everything can make you happy if you let it. Be unconditionally happy. Happy for no reason. Enjoy everything as it is, and watch your world change.

Ask Yourself: What If You Let Yourself Be Happy Without External Circumstances?

_____

_____

_____

_____

_____

_____

_____

_____

Chapter Eight

What If All Your Dreams Came True Right Now?

If all your dreams came true right now, what would be left to do? Sure you could enjoy them for a bit, but then what? People fail to realize it's having dreams that motivates them, it's having dreams that pushes them. If you had everything you wanted, you'd have nothing left to chase after.

There's an ancient story that tells us why creation exists. It says that, at one point, before the birth of our universe, we were full. We were full of desires, love, and joy. Sated with instant satisfaction and wholeness until we became aware that we were weren't giving it to ourselves. At that point, we split and the universe had its Big Bang. Since then, we've been playing a game of creation. Finding our way through creating our own fulfillment. You see, according to this story, we once had all our dreams come true in an instant. What we longed for then was to manifest it on our own.

The truth is, we don't want all our dreams to come true right now. We want to work for them, strive for them, and earn them ourselves, one at a time. That is the joy of our human experience.

Ask Yourself: What If All Your Dreams Came True Right Now?

_____

_____

_____

_____

_____

_____

_____

_____

CHAPTER NINE

What If Life Is Happening For You , Not Against You?

Life happens. Each day we wake up and life happens. Things transpire all day in each of our lives. The kids wake up cranky and screaming, or peaceful and calm. We're late to work, or early. We get fired, or we get promoted. Find the love of our life, or get a divorce. Not everything is always this extreme, but we get just a bit of all of it. I've had ups and downs all day, every day, and so have others. That is life.

What if it was all happening for us? What if even the downs of life were ups for us? Just think for a minute, that the universe is conspiring for our greatest lesson in each moment? To believe that each and every one of our life's moments is happening for our benefit? How might your days go if you actually felt that way? If every time you were stuck in traffic, you knew it was for you? If that breakup was a benefit to you? If getting fired was your victory for the day? All of life's ups and downs are here to serve you? They are yours to learn and grow from if you can view them that way. Each has a lesson encoded within it, just waiting to be dis- covered. Open your mind, open your heart, give yourself patience and space, then see your life as unfolding for your benefit. The universe is always working for you.

Ask Yourself: What If Life Is Happening For You , Not Against You?

_____

_____

_____

_____

_____

_____

_____

_____

CHAPTER TEN

What If The World Is A Reflection Of You And Only You Can Change It?

It's a big world out there, over seven billion people and counting. Seven continents with 196 independent nations. What if it depended on you? What if the only way to change anything in this world started with you? Byron Katie once said, "The world is a reflection of your mind." I believe that to be true. There's an age-old saying that states: "As within, so without." What if changing yourself is the only way to change the world? The truth is, we must save ourselves first. When I experienced oneness with all life, I knew it was all me. Not Corey Gladwell, the individual, but the greater me, the one observing me. The only thing that needs to be changed is me. The only person who needs to be saved is me. Read these last two sentences as if speaking for yourself. Only you need to change. No one and nothing else.

As Mahatma Gandhi said, "Be the change you wish to see in the world." It is only you who can change anything, by changing yourself. The world is simply a reflection of you. All of its joy and all of its turmoil. Everything is simply you. Change yourself, change the world. The greatest gift you can give the world is the most authentic version of yourself.

Ask Yourself: What If The World Is A Reflection Of You And Only You Can Change It?

_____

_____

_____

_____

_____

_____

_____

_____

CHAPTER ELEVEN

What If You Had All The Money In The World?
Then What Would You Want?

People spend much of their time focused on making money. They say we spend 65% of our time with our coworkers. That more than half of our waking lives is spent working is incredible. We go to school to get a job (hopefully a career), to pay for a house and pay for our kids to go to school, so they can get a job, and do the same thing. We spend all this time chasing wealth, in one form or another, to pay for things we don't get time to use.

What if you had all the money in the world? What if you had a limitless supply of income? Then what would you do? Come up with your list; not so much a material object list, but a time list. You can only buy so many cars, clothes, and homes before you, too, are bored with them. Think more on what you would do with the freedom of time, with the ability to allocate your ever decreasing commodity of time. How would you spend your days? The whole point of income is to have time later to spend it on what you want. What if you can have all the money? A better question might be: Why do you want money? Find those reasons and decide today that you will do them. It may take time, but what is a few years in comparison to the rest of your life? What if you let go of the need to have money to enjoy your time and just spend your time doing things that you would do if you had the money?

Ask Yourself: What If You Had All The Money In The World? Then What Would You Want?

_____

_____

_____

_____

_____

_____

_____

_____

CHAPTER TWELVE

What If Getting What You Think You Want Will Actually Make You Unhappy?

We walk through life assuming we know what we want. If only this job would be this way or that person would act differently. We have a list of changes we think would make us happy or happier. But what if that weren't the case? The reality is: If you're not willing to work for it, day in and day out for years, then you don't really want it. To get too easily what you think you want would be a temporary high with an eventual come-down, leaving you in an even bigger hole than before. What is worth working the rest of your life for to make you happy? A job change, a new car, a different relationship? All these things are external. To be truly satisfied, you need to look within. What will fill your soul? What would make you whole, complete, and full of peace? That's worth seeking. That in itself can never leave you unhappy.

Ask Yourself: What If Getting What You Think You Want Will Actually Make You Unhappy?

Chapter THIRTEEN

What If Who You Are To Become Is Greater Than You Can Imagine You Wan t To Be?

We all have this ideal version of ourselves, this perfect person we want to live up to. What if who you will become is beyond that image? Think back to when you were five years old. Even then you had an idea of who you wanted to be. At that point, it was probably a police officer or an astronaut, but the idea was there. We took in information and concepts from school, family, and friends, and began to form our future self in our minds. As we grew up, things changed. What we thought was cool changed. What we saw in others changed. Our likes and dislikes changed. But our future self- concept didn't go away. It only evolved. Flash forward until today and the same is true. This time it may not be so much about being something as a profession but as an inner self-reflection, more in-tangible; Things like loving, compassion, persistence, caring.

What if the best version of yourself is beyond your imagination? What if it's not the idea of perfection you have in your mind, but is far beyond perfect? Don't limit your future by imposing concept after concept on it. Don't shortchange yourself by holding onto an image of what you currently think you should be. Let go of all concepts of perfection. Fully accept yourself and the unknown perfection of your future. Who you become may be beyond your capacity to imagine.

Ask Yourself: What If Who You Are To Become Is Greater Than You Can Imagine You Wan t To Be?

_____

_____

_____

_____

_____

_____

_____

CHAPTER FOURTEEN

What If Your Life's Work Is Something Beyond Your Ability To Perceive?

People often think of their life's work as something they do for a living. What if that's not the case? I believe it is our limited perception that keeps us from seeing this. We search for the career or the business we will start in order to fulfill ourselves or find our purpose. What if it is the simple act of being who we are that is your life's work. As Gandhi said, "Your life is your message". Doing what you're doing is your life's work. Being the friend, child, parent, lover, or coworker you are is your life's work. Are you representing your life's work the way you would want? If not, then show the world who you truly are. Be the manifestation of what you want to present to the world. This is your life's work.

Ask Yourself: What If Your Life's Work Is Something Beyond Your Ability To Perceive?

_____

_____

_____

_____

_____

_____

_____

CHAPTER FIFTEEN

What if this is it, and nothing more will happen externally in your life?

Here you are, in this moment. This is your life. Are you satisfied? Are you fulfilled? What if this is it? What if nothing more happens? How does that question feel? That feeling will give you your answer. Can you learn to accept your life exactly how it is? You must first accept it, then take action. If your current reality is not what fulfills you, then take action. Take action to change your personality. Change who you are from the inside. Then everything else will change. As Dr. Joe Dispenza says, "A new personality creates a new personal reality." It is you who must change first. You must become the person inside that equals the life you want on the out- side. Use your answer to change the inner workings of your mind and heart. Then your life will transform externally.

Ask Yourself: What if this is it, and nothing more will happen externally in your life?

_____

_____

_____

_____

_____

_____

_____

CHAPTER SIXTEEN

What if being in a bad relationship is your fault?

Many people have suffered from at least one bad relationship. I, at least, have yet to meet someone who hasn't had at least one. What if you're currently in one and it's your fault? You see the truth is, it's your choice. They say you date at the level of your self-esteem. Your relationship is a reflection of you. If your partner is lying, cheating, or hurting you, it is what you are allowing. What we allow will continue. You must hold yourself higher than that. The truth is love is an action. It's not what you say, but what you do, that shows love. If their actions are not loving, then they don't love you. If you stay, allowing it to continue, then re- ally you don't love yourself. Your action to stay in an unhealthy relationship is telling you that you don't love yourself enough to do what's best for you. Are you loving yourself today? Are your relationships reflecting what you truly want?

Ask Yourself: What if being in a bad relationship is your fault?

_____

_____

_____

_____

_____

_____

_____

CHAPTER SEVENTEEN

What if your experiences weren't at all what you thought they were?

Do you ever to stop to consider that maybe the way you thought an experience went was not how it went? Every day we have circumstances, conversations, meetings, hang out with friends and lovers, all the while assuming we know how those experiences went. We think, "Aw, that was a great time" or "Wow, that was bad." All of these are merely our version of the experience. Only our truth is what we see and feel. This dissonance between what happens in our mind's lens and others' can be close or very far apart. We can't assume that our experience is the only version.

If we are aware enough, we need only ask another person a few questions to find out how they experienced the same situation. What may have been bad for us may been good for them. What may have been uncomfortable to us may have fit right in their comfort zone. We do not know what another person experiences but we make an assumption based on our own likes, dislikes, and biases. We mustn't rob them of the value of their experience. Simply acknowledge that what you experience is only true for you. Give others the freedom to have and learn from their own experience and if you want to know about it, simply ask.

Ask Yourself: What if your experiences weren't at all what you thought they were?

_____

_____

_____

_____

_____

_____

_____

_____

CHAPTER EIGHTEEN

What if that conversation wasn't true?

Just as our experiences are not the same as everyone else's, so are our conversations. Every day we have conversations with our family and friends, spouses and coworkers, but what if they didn't go the way we thought they did? Each person we speak with, we must realize, has their own definition for each word used. What they define as good, bad, healthy, truthful, etc. varies by person. You may leave a conversation thinking you understand their words, when in fact you don't. You may simple understand your definition of the words they used. Someone may be spilling their heart out to you and you would have no idea. The degree to which people open up in honesty and love can change drastically for each person. Be cautious when making presumptions about what someone is communicating. Take a moment to pause and truly comprehend what is being said and what is not being said. When in doubt, ask more questions to get more clarification. It is much better to ask more than to understand less. After all, you would want to be truly understood yourself, so give that to others.

Ask Yourself: What if that conversation wasn't true?

_____

_____

_____

_____

_____

_____

_____

_____

CHAPTER NINETEEN

What if you didn't believe your thoughts?

To some that may sound like an attack on who they are. People at- tach so deeply to their thoughts that they define themselves. What if you could question your thoughts? What if you didn't believe them? I hope we can all agree that not every thought we have is true, so if that's the case, then what about those thoughts we hold as truth? What about those beliefs that we so strongly hold to? History has proven to us that people will go to war over thoughts, kill for them, even create genocide over them. They can tell us that someone is better or worse than us, good or evil, should live or die, which are all just their opinion. What is the thought you've been having that you could do without? How might you feel if you didn't believe this thought? How might your level of thought, your level of emotion, and your general state of being change if this thought was lifted from your mind? Ask yourself that. Imagine life without that thought.

No one is forcing us to believe anything or think anything. If there is one thing in life we have control over, it is what goes on in our minds. Take your power back. Remove that thought and watch how much easier your life gets. Experience freedom in that moment.

Ask Yourself: What if you didn't believe your thoughts?

_____

_____

_____

_____

_____

_____

_____

_____

CHAPTER TWENTY

What if you didn't have thoughts?

L et's take it one step further. Let's imagine your life without thoughts at all. Can you do that? If we take away thoughts entirely, clear our minds, as is done during some forms of meditation, how might we be? For starters, there'd be no more judgment. Literally the end of judgment. No more biases, likes or dislikes. No more stories of our lives to tell of how hard or bad things have been. Just you. No filter, separation, identification, just pure you. Free your mind. How might it feel to not have to tell your story over and over again? How might it feel to not have to judge anymore? How might it feel to be free of incessant thinking always telling you what to like, want, crave, desire, have, lack, or change? Just freedom to be, just freedom to feel, without blame, just freedom to live, without limits.

Ask Yourself: What if you didn't have thoughts?

_____

_____

_____

_____

_____

_____

_____

_____

CHAPTER TWENTY-ONE

What if you didn't have the story of your life?

No matter what age we are, we all have our story. We combined our perception of each experience throughout our lives into one long narrative, with us as the star of the show. What if we didn't have our story? What if all that we've told ourselves isn't truth? What if we let go of it completely? Each experience we've had, as we remember it, is merely our version. We only know what the filter of our perceptual lens has provided us. What if we ac- knowledge that the how and what of our lives isn't exactly the truth. What if we let go of it completely? If we can stop telling the story altogether, we can find freedom. What is the use of repeating story after story to total strangers, or even to those we know? It seems to be the people we bond with the most are the ones that agree with our version of the story, or at least let us tell it to them over and over again.

Our sense of self is so wrapped up in our story that when it is questioned, we get defensive. What if our old story no longer identifies us? Our story could simply be, "I am here now." Just that simple. No more past, no more future, no more projection, just this loving, unfiltered moment.

Ask Yourself: What if you didn't have the story of your life?

_____

_____

_____

_____

_____

_____

_____

Chapter twenty-two

What if you were free to be anyone you wanted?

You were born pure without ideas, concepts, beliefs, or a personality. Life continued on up until today, creating who you are in this moment. Are you who you want to be? Do you love the way you want, think what you want, feel what you want? Are your actions aligned with what you want to represent to the world? If not, then what is stopping you from being that person? We all have a personality that has been developed over the years, but it's within our power to change that. In reality, it is all we have control over. If you could be anyone you wanted, who would that person be? What would they think? How would they feel? How would they love? What actions would they take each day? Decide who you want to be then spend your days becoming that person. You're free to be anyone you want to be.

Ask Yourself: What if you were free to be anyone you wanted?

_____

_____

_____

_____

_____

_____

_____

CHAPTER TWENTY-THREE

What if needing nothing attracts everything?

We all have our list of desires, wants, and wishes. What if it is our longing for it that keeps it away from us? As long as we feel separate, as long as we feel we need it, our craving keeps it from us. Needing nothing attracts everything. Accept that you are all that exists. Accept that perfect health is yours. Wealth is you. Love is what you're made of. Once you do, then everything is yours because everything is you. There's no law that says you have to be unhealthy, unhappy, or poor. There's no destiny in that. There's no God making that happen. You, and you alone, are responsible. Your belief system is the only thing holding you back. Embrace, accept, acknowledge, and believe that you are all that exists. That you will never have to want for anything again. Needing nothing truly attracts everything.

Ask Yourself: What if needing nothing attracts everything?

_____

_____

_____

_____

_____

_____

_____

CHAPTER TWENTY-FOUR

What if your greatest accomplishment is just being alive?

You're born whole. You're born complete. You're born perfect. There is nothing in this world that you need to complete you. Nothing that to stop you going into the world and doing what makes you happy. Your greatest accomplishment is being alive. Everything else is a bonus. There is nothing you need to do, finish, create, or become to make you any more complete. You can have the dream job, relationship, house, and life, but need to hold on to the knowledge that you're the greatest gift the universe has ever created. You're its physical manifestation in the flesh. You're the universe discovering itself as itself, its eyes to see, its ears to hear. There is nothing you need to prove to anyone, including yourself, for this to be true. You are absolutely perfect in this exact moment. With that knowledge, you can have, or be anything you want. It is already you.

Ask Yourself: What if your greatest accomplishment is just being alive?

_____

_____

_____

_____

_____

_____

_____

Chapter twenty-five

What if what you think is true is a lie you tell yourself?

How much do you know is true? Think about it for a moment. How much do you really know to be absolutely, without question, true? The reality is there is not a lot we can prove to be true when it comes down to how we think and feel. Of course the truth is we are thinking and feeling it, so we believe it to be true. What if what you tell yourself is a lie? What if what you think and feel isn't true? We doubt what others think and feel, so why wouldn't we question our own thoughts and feelings? Cognitive dissonance makes it very hard for us to accept a view that contradicts our current one. It is our perception that fosters our current belief system. Anything that disagrees or contradicts it has a hard time finding its way in. Knowing that you could have multiple built-up lies in your view of yourself and others, when confronted with the truth, do you flat out ignore it? Give yourself the mental and emotional space to find the truth by first accepting that you may not know it. Once you do that, you can allow room for the truth to come in.

Ask Yourself: What if what you think is true is a lie you tell yourself?

_____

_____

_____

_____

_____

_____

_____

CHAPTER TWENTY-SIX

What if you owned your emotions?

However you're feeling right now, whatever that emotion is, what if you could control it? Just imagine for a moment that you feel whole, full of love, joy, and passion. Ecstatic for life and what it has to offer. Just hold that for a moment. You suddenly can have all the confidence in the world. You feel infinite and limitless in your excitement for life. What if you could pull this feeling up whenever you wanted? Every time you had a single doubt or worry, you could instantly know that everything would work out perfectly for you just by declaring it. Every moment you felt angry or hurt, you could make a decision to feel love and forgiveness. Every sad moment of longing could be turned into a joyous reverence for life.

What if every emotion you ever wanted to feel was at the touch of your fingertips, was on demand in any moment? You truly are the only one who can make yourself feel anything. No one else can make you feel good or bad, happy or sad, loved or rejected. These, like all of our emotions, are completely in our control. We must give power to and agree with what someone else says or does for to it to affect us. When you acknowledge the power you have to own and operate your body of emotions, you are set free from slavery to others. When you have an emotion like anger, it is only you who suffers. No matter how much yelling, screaming, orcrying you do, only you have to live with that inside you. In those moments, what will serve you most is surrender, space, and the acknowledgment that a better emotion can take its place. This does not mean denial of how we feel. It simply means pause, then transmute the energy into a more useful flow. What will best serve you? What will help heal you? What would make you whole? It is your choice, always.

Ask Yourself: What if you owned your emotions?

_____

_____

_____

_____

_____

_____

_____

CHAPTER TWENTY-SEVEN

What if you could change your mind about anything, anytime?

Your job, your lovers, your friends, your families, your kids, your coworkers ... Do you have positive thoughts about each and every one of those? Be honest. Not that it is by any means a requirement to be positive, but what does the negative thought process do to you? Once you begin down the road of ungrateful, unappreciative, unhappy thoughts about one person, place, or thing, it begins to slowly seep into the rest of your world. What if you could just change your mind? What if that person that bothers you no longer did? What if that position at work didn't frustrate you? Disclaimer: This does not mean that we accept unhealthy people or places into our lives. No. I'm not saying allow them to be around you or to continue to be in an unhealthy environment. I'm saying stop letting it rent space in your mind. Change your thoughts at any time to a have a more useful, peaceful mind. Unplug the cord, detach from the mental chatter. Take your power back and re- focus it on yourself. These are your thoughts,this is your mind. Don't let anything or anyone in who doesn't make it better.

Ask Yourself: What if you could change your mind about anything, anytime?

_____

_____

_____

_____

_____

_____

_____

Chapter twenty-eight

What if you let go completely of being in control of your life?

What do you really have control over? Can you control other people? What they think, feel, say, or do? No. Can you control every- thing at work or at home? No. You sure can try. You can frustrate yourself all day and night trying to control things that you really can't. When you boil it down, all you have control over is yourself. What you think, feel, say, and do. You and only you. Everything else is frustration waiting to happen. You are in control of what you think and feel. You have control over your words and your actions.

The best you can do is decide what you want out of your life. Choose the relationships you want, the work you want, then voice exactly what you want to those in your life. Tell them how you want to be treated. Once again, you can't control them but you can control yourself. If those in your life don't want to treat you that way, then remove yourself from them. Remove yourself from any- thing and anyone who doesn't treat you the way you want. That is what you have control over. Let go of trying to control anything or anyone else in your life. That's when you get all the power back. That's when you stop wasting energy on things that are beyond you. Focus completely on what you can control, which is you and you alone. Raise your standards, and if people truly want to stay in your life, they will rise up to meet them.

Ask Yourself: What if you let go completely of being in control of your life?

_____

_____

_____

_____

_____

_____

_____

_____

CHAPTER TWENTY-NINE

What if you spend a year following signs from the universe to decide your future?

Do you ever wonder what decision to make? Should I stay at this job or be in this relationship? Should I move out of town? We all have these life-altering decisions throughout our life, but what if we took our cues from the universe? Imagine you have one of these decisions to make. It's weighing on your mind and heart daily. Now take a step back and look at it objectively. Separate your thoughts and emotions from it and surrender it to the universe. Give it up completely. Allow some time but be open to signs. A good rule of thumb is three signs. The truth is, deep down, you've made the decision already. You just haven't accepted it yet. Allow the universe to show you your choice a few times then you will know it has been made. This is how we act through surrender. We give it up and allow the answers within us to be revealed to us. How might your life change if you practice surrender in your daily decisions?

Ask Yourself: What if you spend a year following signs from the universe to decide your future?

_____

_____

_____

_____

_____

_____

_____

CHAPTER THIRTY

What if you surrendered to each moment of what life brought to you?

Surrender. A word with a powerful action behind it. Deep sur- render to what is, can transform one's life. Can we truly surrender to each moment life brings us? Surrender does not mean "no action." Surrender means fully accepting each moment as it is. Then, and only then, should we take action. Only after we have surrendered, accepted, and can love what is, will we take appropriate action. Once surrender has taken place, the moment no longer has power over us. The person, place, or thing that we are faced with has no power to control our internal state. At that moment, we are free. We have taken our power back and we can then take action from a place of peace; where true, positive, and powerful actions can stem.

Ask Yourself: What if you surrendered to each moment of what life brought to you?

_____

_____

_____

_____

_____

_____

CHAPTER THIRTY-ONE

What if every conversation you have, no matter how small, is really for your greatest good?

We go to the post office, wait in line. The person behind us asks how we're doing? Do we leave it at "good" or do we expand further? Dive in and really connect with this human being. Who knows what life experience they have? Who knows what wisdom they may bring to us if only we allow ourselves to open up to it? Why only think of the huge moments as signs from the universe? Why not realize that everything is there to assist us if only we would let it. I've had the most profound insights from a simple conversation. I've had total strangers tell me a story that reshaped my outlook. The most unimpressive sentence has evolved my love for my family. You don't know where the next answer will come from, but when you open up, it may come to you through the most unexpected person or place.

Ask Yourself: What if every conversation you have, no matter how small, is really for your greatest good?

_____

_____

_____

_____

_____

_____

_____

CHAPTER THIRTY-TWO

What If All Your Problems Disappeared?

What if you didn't have a struggle? We have become addicted to our struggle. We complain about our jobs, money, relationships, kids, parents, friends, and so on. We have the story of struggle. Every time someone asks how we're doing, we go on and on about our list of problems. The story of struggle has become our addiction. It's now a part of who we are. This part of you must die in order to be free of your struggle.

Ask yourself who you would be without your story? Who you would be without your problems? How would you feel, how would you think? What would your new story be, if you had no problems in your life? Let this be your new outlook. Every time you catch yourself complaining, just stop and ask yourself, "Do I really want to be happy? Do I really want to be well off, or broke? Do I really want a healthy relationship, or a toxic one?" Let go of your addiction to the struggle and the story you create about it. Then create a new story of your life.

Ask Yourself: What If All Your Problems Disappeared?

_____

_____

_____

_____

_____

_____

_____

Chapter thirty-three

What If You Let Go of Power?

Power is so seductive. We get a little bit and most people begin to crave more. What if by letting go of power, you gain all the power. You see, while you search to hold onto power, you're actually powerless. You're at the will of that which you want to have power over. When you realize that needing nothing will attract everything, you can simply let go. Holding onto power is exhausting and only leads to pain. While letting go of power releases all tension and gives you all the power back. You're no longer needing to control or manipulate people, places, or things. You are free from those you wish to hold power over. You are set free. The power is truly found in relinquishing the need for any power at all. Nothing owns you, nothing controls you. You have it all by simply letting go. Power is what creates wars, ruins governments, fails marriages, and removes any chance of success in relationships, be they personal or business. Letting go of power is what gives you power back over yourself.

Ask Yourself: What If You Let Go of Power?

_____

_____

_____

_____

_____

_____

_____

CHAPTER THIRTY-FOUR

What If You Accepted Death as a Natural Part of Life?

How often do you think about death? About your own death or of the people in your life dying? It's not a subject most of us want to touch with a ten-foot pole. In all reality though, it is a natural part of life. Everyone is born, lives, and dies. We have yet to discover the fountain of youth or a pill for immortality. So what if we accepted death as a natural part of life? What if we spent our days with the awareness that, one day, it will all end? I frequently step into this mindset and feel a profound sense of gratitude for my life and those who fill it.

Spend a moment simply acknowledging those with whom you share a bond. That one day they won't be here. Take a moment to tell them what they truly mean to you, before it is too late. I was told once that the dead receive more flowers than the living, because regret is a stronger emotion than appreciation. Don't wait 'til it's too late. Don't have regrets. Become grateful for your limited time here on earth and the rare moments you get with the ones you love.

Ask Yourself: What If You Accepted Death as a Natural Part of Life?

_____

_____

_____

_____

_____

_____

CHAPTER THIRTY-FIVE

What If You Embrace Change as a Friend, Here to Guide You to Your Greatest Good?

We've all heard the saying, "The only constant is change." We know things will change yet why do we resist it so much? Because we are creatures of habit. We love our comfort zones, regardless of whether they make us unhappy or not. But what if we embrace change? What if we saw change as a friend here to bring us to our greatest good? How much more excited and passionate would we be, if we jumped for joy at the opportunity to change?

Growth comes from change. We must remember that. If we want growth in any area of our lives, we must be willing to change. We must embrace change as a friend, here to guide us to our greatest good. I was told that we must get comfortable being uncomfortable. Want your relationship to grow? Embrace change. Want your career to grow? Embrace change. Want to improve your health? Embrace change. All areas in which we want to grow begin with a change. We must recognize that even when things seem to be falling apart, they are simply changing, to make room for growth.

Ask Yourself: What If You Embrace Change as a Friend, Here to Guide You to Your Greatest Good?

_____

_____

_____

_____

_____

_____

_____

CHAPTER THIRTY-SIX

What If You Let Go of the Idea of Perfection for Yourself and Others?

Expectations kill relationships. Believing another person should show up the way you want them to will leave you bitter. Yes we can have standards of how we deserve to be treated, yet we must not put perfectionism onto our relationships. How would it feel if no one expected you to be perfect? If the people in your life loved you and always forgave you for not being perfect? What kind of joy would be brought into your life if you were free to just live and let others live?

If you truly want acceptance and forgiveness from others, then you must start with yourself. You must begin to accept and for- give yourself for not being perfect, then allow others the same loving grace. This freedom can bring you the joy of realizing you and everyone else are perfectly imperfect. We are humans. We are great, and we are weak. We are beautiful, and we have moments of ugliness. Yet in the end we love, and that is all that matters.

Ask Yourself: What If You Let Go of the Idea of Perfection for Yourself and Others?

_____

_____

_____

_____

_____

_____

_____

CHAPTER THIRTY-SEVEN

What If You Knew Everything Would Work Out?

How often are we driven by fear and worry? We battle that ancient voice in our minds that tells us we must worry, or it will all fall apart. What if we found a place, deep down inside, that was confident that everything would work out? If we access this place and live from this place, how might we act instead? How would you act during a breakup if you knew true love never fades? How would you act at your job if you knew your life purpose was waiting? What would your decisions look like if you knew without a doubt that it would all work out exactly, or even better, than you wanted?

Just think for a moment. Take away all the fear and worry, then replace it with confident knowledge, profound love, deep-seated trust, and a sense of peace. What would your next choice be? How might your life unfold if only you let the good in?

Ask Yourself: What If You Knew Everything Would Work Out?

_____

_____

_____

_____

_____

_____

_____

Chapter thirty-eight

What If Every Time You Judge Another You Are Really Judging Yourself?

Judgment. We all have been guilty of it at one point or another. We see something we dislike in another and we compare it to the behavior we deem acceptable. What if by doing that, we are truly judging ourselves? You see, the behavior we dislike in another is a reflection of a part of ourselves we are disowning. We are saying to ourselves that we can't accept that. That we can't accept them. This lack of acceptance shuts our hearts off from accepting ourselves.

We are not perfect in every single way, so to not allow others to have imperfections prevents us from allowing ourselves our own imperfections. Only when you accept others can you fully accept yourself. It's judgement of them that brings up the judge within us, which makes us begin to disown a part of who we are. We must decide to accept love and allow others to be who they are without judgement if we are ever going to be free of our own selves to live.

Ask Yourself: What If Every Time You Judge Another You Are Really Judging Yourself?

_____

_____

_____

_____

_____

_____

Chapter thirty-nine

What If You Could Create Anything You Desired?

Many of us already create our reality over and over again. We are just creating it unconsciously. In our attempts to manipulate and control what is happening in our lives, we manufacture fear-based results. We doom and gloom all day and guess what? Doom and gloom show up. What if you could use this power of creation for our deepest desires? What if you could create anything you desired?

The truth is you can. I know because I have done it myself and taught many others to do it as well. The secret is to let go of fear. The secret is to let go of control and manipulation. Instead of coming from a place of forced outcomes, come from a place of unconditional love. Come from a place of deep knowledge, of surrender to your highest good, of confidence in your highest self. You see we must let go of who we think we are. We must embrace change as our guide, we must accept the unknown as the place where all possibilities exist. Your future self will thank you for taking the leap.

Decide what you want. Feel it as if it's yours everyday, and take steps with pure intention. The act of wanting itself is what creates the lack within you; to think you are separate from it. Do not want for anything. Instead acknowledge that you already have it and accept it and know it deep down.

Ask Yourself: What If You Could Create Anything You Desired?

_____

_____

_____

_____

_____

_____

_____

CHAPTER FORTY

What If Your Life Has Been Designed for Your Highest Good?

Excitement, failure, love, loss. Everyone's life has a mix of experiences. What if your life has been designed for your highest good? Everything has prepared you for this moment, that has landed you with my book in your hands. Every single thing that has led to this single question. All of it may not seem like a blessing, but it has made you into a person who's looking for more and that is the greatest gift you can have. You are in a place where you are asking questions and with each question, your awareness grows. As your awareness grows, your consciousness deepens, and as I've said, it is the depth of your consciousness that will determine your capacity for experience.

At the end of your life, you will have only that, your experience. Truly your life has been designed for your highest good. What will you do now? How far do you want to go? How deep do you want to take it?

Ask Yourself: What If Your Life Has Been Designed for Your Highest Good?

_____

_____

_____

_____

_____

_____

_____

CHAPTER FORTY-ONE

What If You Were Happier Because of That Loss?

Sometimes getting what we think we want isn't always the best. That dream, relationship, job, or goal may inadvertently make us unhappy. We can't always see this before we get it. What if you were happier because of that loss? What if not getting what you think you want, will actually make your life better? Be open mind- ed. Welcome a change to your plans. Be free to know that life may take you in an even better direction than you may have had planned. Life is funny that way in that it knows us better than we know ourselves. We may fight, kicking and screaming, yet end up in a much better place after we let go.

The only way to test this is simple. Is it forced or coming with ease? If it's forced, then it's not meant to be. If it comes with ease or a little hard work, then it's meant for you. When things are for your highest good, life will flow for you and with you.

Ask Yourself: What If You Were Happier Because of That Loss?

_____

_____

_____

_____

_____

_____

_____

_____

CHAPTER FORTY-TWO

What If Every Person You Met Was a Part of You that You Haven't Met Yet?

From family and friends to a stranger at the store, everyone is a version of us. Each person in the world is unique. Each person has their own personality, likes and dislikes, interests and hobbies. But what if everyone was simply a version of ourselves we haven't met yet? You see we are all connected. Each one of us is one being experiencing itself as seven and a half billion unique personalities. Every person you meet is a version of you.

What if you walked through life with this awareness? What if you could learn something about yourself from every person you met? Everyone has something to teach us about ourselves. The traits we determine are simply admirable we wish to have more of, or less. Other traits we despise and those are our shadow self that we must make peace with. If something in someone's personality bothers you, then it is a part of you that you have denied. Embrace it, accept it, learn to love it.

Similarly, if you find yourself attracted to traits in others, know that those are the traits in you that you love. Enjoy those and celebrate them inside yourself. Know that each person you meet is a reflection of who you are. Learn patience for them as you would want for yourself.

Ask Yourself: What If Every Person You Met Was a Part of You that You Haven't Met Yet?

_____

_____

_____

_____

_____

_____

_____

_____

CHAPTER FORTY-THREE

What If Loving Someone You Hate is the Only Way to Truly Love Yourself?

How can one love and hate simultaneously? Having hate inside of us snuffs out the love we have. The feeling of hatred for another only serves to poison the love inside us. When you have hatred for another, you are preventing love for all others including your- self. Your love is only as deep as your hate for another. You must let go of this hatred in order to truly love yourself. When you find peace for the ones you hate, you will simultaneously find love for yourself. It is only through forgiveness that we find acceptance. It is only through acceptance that we find peace. It is only when we find peace, that we allow love.

Ask Yourself: What If Loving Someone You Hate is the Only Way to Truly Love Yourself?

_____

_____

_____

_____

_____

_____

_____

CHAPTER FORTY-FOUR

What If We Take the Safe Route and Fail Anyway?

Go to school, get a job, buy a house, get married, have kids. That's what you're supposed to do, right? Not saying those things are not fulfilling, but are you doing them because you really want to? Even if we play it safe, go to the right school, or get the steady job, we can still fail. So playing it safe isn't always safe. True freedom comes from following your heart, from following your dreams. Even if you fail, simply learn from it and try again. You can fail being safe, so why not chase after your deepest desires and find out what's at the end of the rainbow. Be the butterfly.

What If You Said Yes Instead of No?

Every time we have to make a decision, we tend to weigh it out. Usually it comes down to how we feel. "I don't feel like it," is a response we've all heard. But what if we said yes instead of no? What if we took that scary leap to move, change careers, or go to that new place? You see our ego wants us to stay comfortable. Our ego wants to stay with what's known. It takes effort to step out into the unknown.

What if you said yes to the new promotion? What if you said yes to that trip? What if the love of your life is waiting for you there? What if you meet your new best friend? Your freedom could be one decision away. Your dream life could be waiting for you, and all you have to do is have the courage to say yes.

Ask Yourself: What If We Take the Safe Route and Fail Anyway?

_____

_____

_____

_____

_____

_____

CHAPTER FORTY-FIVE

What If You Said Yes Instead of No?

Every time we have to make a decision, we tend to weigh it out. Usually it comes down to how we feel. "I don't feel like it," is a response we've all heard. But what if we said yes instead of no? What if we took that scary leap to move, change careers, or go to that new place? You see our ego wants us to stay comfortable. Our ego wants to stay with what's known. It takes effort to step out into the unknown.

What if you said yes to the new promotion? What if you said yes to that trip? What if the love of your life is waiting for you there? What if you meet your new best friend? Your freedom could be one decision away. Your dream life could be waiting for you, and all you have to do is have the courage to say yes.

Ask Yourself: What If You Said Yes Instead of No?

_____

_____

_____

_____

_____

_____

CHAPTER FORTY-SIX

What If You Had No Problems to Solve?

Isn't it funny how we always seem to have something to work on, a problem to solve or something inside of us to fix? Every time you turn around, there's a new bill or drama with a friend or some new diagnosis you must fix inside yourself. What if you had no problems to solve? What if there was nothing wrong? What if you woke up tomorrow with nothing to do, with nothing to solve, completely at peace, and life in every way was perfect? What would you do?

You see, our ego wants to survive just as we do. Our ego will die when we find peace. Peace has no need for an ego. So our sub- conscious mind manufactures problems to solve, things to fix. We create dramas and stories to keep our ego alive. Our obsessions, our fights, our judgements ... All of them stem from the ego's need to survive. Spend an entire day doing nothing. Solving nothing, worrying about or fixing nothing, and watch how crazy your ego will go. It will create thoughts of fear and worry. It will manufacture anxiety. None of it is real. Nothing needs to be done. You are complete and whole in this moment.

Ask Yourself: What If You Had No Problems to Solve?

_____

_____

_____

_____

_____

_____

_____

_____

CHAPTER FORTY-SEVEN

What If No One is Coming to Save You but You?

We all in our own way want to be saved, to be rescued from our pain, our loss, or even our job. But what if no one is coming? What if the only person who will save you is yourself? There's a great freedom in taking 100% responsibility for your life. There's a sense of pride, a deep knowledge, and a profound joy in owning your own life. Many of us want to blame, label, judge, or complain about what has happened to us. We want to deflect our choices. We outsource our emotions. We put off what we know is in our hearts. All the while, waiting secretly for someone or some bit of magic to make it all different.

After I lost everything, I had a hard time with this. I didn't have anyone to blame. When I finally came to terms with the fact that my life is my own, I found true freedom. No longer do you have to ask for permission to do what you know is in your heart. You're the savior you've been waiting for. You are the hero in the story of your life. You must save yourself.

Great expectations. They tend to trap us in a belief of shoulds. My family should be this way. My spouse should do this for me. My children should listen. As our expectations for others increase, we simultaneously raise them for ourselves. Expecting others to show up as anyone other than who they are in the moment only causes us pain. We create our own suffering by projecting onto them an image of what we want them to be.

This disillusionment leaves us feeling unsatisfied. When we can learn to allow others to be themselves in the moment, we give that permission to ourselves. How would it feel if no one expected anything of you? How would it feel to be fully accepted for how- ever you are showing up in the moment? Give this feeling to others and you'll be able to give it to yourself as well.

Ask Yourself: What If No One is Coming to Save You but You?

_____

_____

_____

_____

_____

_____

_____

CHAPTER FORTY-EIGHT

What If You Had No Expectations of People?

Great expectations. They tend to trap us in a belief of should. My family should be this way. My spouse should do this for me. My children should listen. As our expectations for others increase, we simultaneously raise them for ourselves. Expecting others to show up as anyone other than who they are in the moment only causes us pain. We create our own suffering by projecting onto them an image of what we want them to be.

This disillusionment leaves us feeling unsatisfied. When we can learn to allow others to be themselves in the moment, we give that permission to ourselves. How would it feel if no one expected anything of you? How would it feel to be fully accepted for how- ever you are showing up in the moment? Give this feeling to others and you'll be able to give it to yourself as well.

Ask Yourself: What If You Had No Expectations of People?

_____

_____

_____

_____

_____

_____

_____

CHAPTER FORTY-NINE

What If Your Life's Purpose is Exactly What You're Doing Right Now?

We search for meaning. We long for purpose. What if your life's purpose is exactly what you're doing right now? Every moment of your life, you've been experiencing. You've been learning, you've been growing. You may not always feel that, but your search has been the destination. Learning to love without being in control. Experiencing loss and how to heal after. Letting go of lower wants for higher needs.

These are life lessons, enough for a single lifetime, yet you've more than likely experienced it all. Your life is your message, as Gandhi would say. You must review, take notes of lessons learned, then through the great gift of giving, share what life has taught you to others. No act is too small, no position insignificant. Your life right now is your purpose.

Ask Yourself: What If Your Life's Purpose is Exactly What You're Doing Right Now?

_____

_____

_____

_____

_____

_____

_____

CHAPTER FIFTY

What If Nothing Needed to Change for You to Be Happy?

Our ideal life always seems to be just around the corner. If only you could get that promotion, that house, that girl or guy. We al- ways seem to be just one step behind perfection. What if nothing needed to change for you to be happy? What if the feeling you think you'll get from acquiring or achieving your desire already exists within you? So you can get there from here.

By that I mean, you must come to find your perfect life, perfect self, or perfect spouse within yourself first. If you keep chasing, you will never find fulfillment. Freedom exists in this now moment. True love is found within your own heart. Believe you are perfect now and perfection will become your reality. If you can't find happiness here, now, then no amount of people, places, or things will satisfy you.

Ask Yourself: What If Nothing Needed to Change for You to Be Happy?

_____

_____

_____

_____

_____

_____

_____

Chapter Fifty-One

What If You Already Are Everything You Wanted to Be?

Many of us long for more. To become healthier, happier, more loving or patient, to be fulfilled completely. But what if you already are everything you wanted to be? What if your best self is waiting within you in this moment? The common way of approaching growth is to add to ourselves. To become more, we think we must add more. But what if it's simply the opposite?

Accessing our highest self is truly an act of letting go. The ability to allow, the process of surrender. We come into this world pure beings of light, completely fulfilled, whole, and perfect. Through our world's way of indoctrination, we are taught to judge, compete, and strive. Now it is our only duty to unlearn, to release what was not ours to begin with. That is where our true self lies. Nothing must be added to you, only relinquished. You already are everything you ever wanted to be. Simply let go of what is not yours to see it.

Ask Yourself: What If You Already Are Everything You Wanted to Be?

_____

_____

_____

_____

_____

_____

_____

CHAPTER FIFTY-TWO

What If Your Life is a Dream that is Yours to Create?

Ever have a dream that you could swear was real? A dream so lucid and vivid you could smell and taste it? That is life. Our lives are a dream. They are a manifestation of our deepest desires or our fears. Are you having an action, a drama, or a nightmare? All we must do is become aware of the fact that each moment is of our own creation, that we are the creators of this dream called life. We are in charge of the unfolding that happens. Each moment is filled with what our hearts and minds decide. Nothing is stopping you from living out your dreams. Nothing is holding you back but your own imagination. When you take full responsibility for your entire life, for every thought and every feeling, you will know freedom. A freedom to create the dream of a lifetime.

Ask Yourself: What If Your Life is a Dream that is Yours to Create?

_____

_____

_____

_____

_____

_____

_____

_____

CHAPTER FIFTY-THREE

What If Letting Go of Control Gave You More Control than You Had?

Control, one of the most sought after things in human history. No one wants to be controlled, yet people are constantly searching for it. What if letting go of control gave you more than you actually had? Releasing control over people, places, and things truly does give it back to yourself. When you can allow life to unfold, without attempting to manipulate it in any way, you will know true power. The power only comes to those that don't long for it. The power that gives you the ability to do what you want, when you want. The control over yourself.

When you let go of trying to force outcomes, you will have peace. Peace to feel your own feelings without them controlling you. Control over your own thoughts without them running you. Power over your own life without the need for others. When you let go of control, you will no longer be dependent on people, your environment, or on anything to give you peace, to make you free. You will have your power, control, freedom, and peace within yourself. You will become yours. You will know true freedom,you will know true peace. You will finally have true control, control over yourself.

Ask Yourself: What If Letting Go of Control Gave You More Control than You Had?

_____

_____

_____

_____

_____

_____

_____

CHAPTER FIFTY-FOUR

What If Loving Others for Who They Are Right Now Was the Only Way to Love Yourself?

Love is one of the most commonly used words. We say it all throughout our lives. Do we truly act on it? Do we love unconditionally? Do we love ourselves? What if loving others for who they are right now is the only way to love ourselves? What if our lack of acceptance is blocking the flow of love for ourselves?

When we force others to become something they're not; when we force them to show up as anything other than who they are in this moment, we are cutting off our own love for ourselves. The blockage of love and expectation of another simultaneously tells our heart that we ourselves are not good enough. We have bad days, too. We aren't always our best selves. We struggle at times just like others. So the lack of compassion and the refusal to love them through their own struggles only tells our heart that we must do the same to ourselves.

Accept, allow, and love others for where they are at. You don't have to be around them, but you can still love them. Allow love for it is your own love that you seek.

Ask Yourself: What If Loving Others for Who They Are Right Now Was the Only Way to Love Yourself?

_____

_____

_____

_____

_____

_____

_____

Chapter Fifty-Five

What If the Universe was Created For You to Have This Exact Moment?

1 4 billion years has gone by since the beginning of time. This entire universe has unfolded, moment after moment. What if it all happened in order for you to experience this exact moment? What if everything has led up to you having these thoughts and feelings, these emotions, for you to have this one single experience?

You are an integral part of each moment. Everything that has happened has led you here. Everything that has unfolded was meant for your highest good. Your experience determines what will come to pass. Your next thought, feeling, and action will determine the course of your life and the direction the universe will take. You are that important.

Once you begin to see how interconnected each experience is, you will know that it has all happened for you. Take a breath in, breathe in life, and know it is happening all for you.

**Ask Yourself: What If the Universe was Created
For You to Have This Exact Moment?**

_____

_____

_____

_____

_____

_____

_____

_____

CHAPTER FIFTY-SIX

What If You Decided Exactly How Life Was Going to Be Before You Got Here?

Many of us question our lives, question our purpose, and the meaning of it all. Why did this happen? Why did that happen? We have a hard time accepting the bad and the good we experience. What if you decided exactly how your life was going to be and how it was going to unfold before you got here? What if everything that has happened, good or bad, was a decision you already made?

It may simply be your job now to understand why you made the decision. What is my highest good? What have I come to learn because of that experience? How has it shaped me into a more fulfilled version of myself? Where has it led me that I may not have otherwise chosen to go? Ask yourself these questions. Come to terms with what life has brought before you. Decide what else you may have to experience in this lifetime. Have peace in the knowledge that your greatest good is always within reach.

Ask Yourself: What If You Decided Exactly How Life Was Going to Be Before You Got Here?

_____

_____

_____

_____

_____

_____

_____

CHAPTER FIFTY-SEVEN

What If You Knew You Were Going to Die Tomorrow?

We've all heard the saying, "Tomorrow's never promised." We toss around these concepts like they're nice ideas, but do any of us take them literally? What if you knew you were going to die tomorrow? What would you do today? What would you say to the ones you love? How would you spend your last 24 hours? Really take this into consideration. Decide right now to not wait until your deathbed to be this way? Make peace with your past. Forgive, share, love, express gratitude, and acknowledge of the love you have.

Why wait until something tragic happens? Why put off giving your best to the people in your life? Why waste another day not living as your best self? This moment is all that exists. Do not put off what you can express today. Share your love, express your deepest feelings, show who you really are to everyone, and spend time how you truly want to spend it. If today was your last day, what would you do?

Ask Yourself: What If You Knew You Were Going to Die Tomorrow?

_____

_____

_____

_____

_____

_____

_____

CHAPTER FIFTY-EIGHT

What If Everything You Thought You Wanted Was Really Programmed in You By Someone Else?

Many of us can remember our dreams dating all the way back to childhood. Hopes, aspirations, wishes we all had. Some of spent our whole lives chasing these dreams. Falling in love with prince charming or our Disney princess, the house with the white picket fence, the beautiful children, the list goes on. Some dreams about jobs, some dreams about life. What if everything you dreamt of was programmed in you? What if your deepest desires only came because they were implanted in your mind?

As young children, we have little say about what we are taught or programmed with. Our parents, family, school, movies, TV, and society dictate to us what makes up most of our subconscious mind. These small nudges fire and wire neurons, fully creating hopes and dreams inside us. Who we want to be, how we want to be seen, the kind of approval we seek ... Take a mental inventory of what's driving you. Are you striving for these things for yourself or for others? If they are for others, they are not meant for you.

What if no one cared what you did? What if everyone already approved of what you wanted? Make sure your dreams are yours and no one else's old programming. Remember, it's not yours. It's theirs.

Ask Yourself: What If Everything You Thought You Wanted Was Really Programmed in You By Someone Else?

_____

_____

_____

_____

_____

_____

_____

CHAPTER FIFTY-NINE

What If All Your Suffering Was Caused By Your Own Mind?

So much goes on in between our ears. Our minds can manufacture the most incredible dreams or our worst nightmares. Sadly, there is a tendency for the latter. We have all experienced fear or sadness, anxiety, guilt, or shame. What if all our suffering was caused by our own mind? Take a moment. Review where your life is right now. Just decide that you are okay with everything exactly how it is. Accept completely where your life is. Who you are, and who is in it. Decide that nothing is wrong. This doesn't mean you can't change or grow, but you can't do that from a place of resistance.

First allow everything in your life to be completely okay as it is. Embrace your life and fill it with love. This is possible for anyone to do. There is someone out there right now who is happier than you with less than you have. Your suffering is a choice. Pain may be real, but suffering is optional. Feel it, see it, love it until it fades away. Your mind wants a reason, but your heart does not need one.

Ask Yourself: What If All Your Suffering Was Caused By Your Own Mind?

_____

_____

_____

_____

_____

_____

_____

CHAPTER SIXTY

What If No One Else is to Blame for Anything but You?

Blame, probably one my least favorite words. Yet it's used in al- most every stressful situation. There was a point in my life when I stopped looking to blame. To stop blaming people, places, situations, or circumstances. I had to find another way. So I replaced the word blame with a new word: responsibility. I decided in that moment that I would no longer blame anything or anyone. I decided that I would take full responsibility for myself and my life.

Since then, everything has changed. In reality, no one is to blame for our lives. Not our parents, society, our boss, no one. When you take on your life as your own, no one can stop you. Realize that nothing is coming to save you. We're not here to get lucky. Life is meant to be created moment by moment. To be a creator, to be the architect of your life, you must own it fully. Once you do, the world will open its doors. Where once you have been stopped, you will now be set free. Empower yourself by owning your life. It is yours to make exactly how you want it.

Ask Yourself: What If No One Else is to Blame for Anything but You?

_____

_____

_____

_____

_____

_____

CHAPTER SIXTY-ONE

What If There Were No Bad Guys?

The other day I was playing with kids and they wanted to be superheroes. So of course, I had to play the bad guy. Nothing out of the normal, the little girl caught my arm and the little boy killed me with his magic sword. I rolled over to pretend to die. Just a normal play time with kids, right?

Almost. The magic moment for me was after I was pretend dead. They looked at each other, they looked over me and said, "Oh no, the bad guy is dead. We'd better bring him back to life." The second I heard that I thought, how often do we get rid of the bad guy in our lives, only to recreate him again? The story of our life's usually based around the same old stories. The hero, the villain, the damsel in distress.

Many times we get rid of the bad guy, i.e. our money problems, our ex, our negative job, etc. only to recreate him again down the road. These repeated patterns of constantly needing a bad guy in our lives, an other if you will, a person or place to blame for our sorrows. Who or what is your bad guy? Do you really want him to be removed from your life? Have you or will you recreate him again and again? We have no need to have a bad guy. There is no enemy. There is no problem. Accept that, and you will be free.

Ask Yourself: What If There Were No Bad Guys?

_____

_____

_____

_____

_____

_____

_____

_____

CHAPTER SIXTY-TWO

What If Forgiveness Isn't for the Other Person?

We're human. We hold grudges, harbor anger, stay lost in resentment, and can take years to forgive. What if forgiveness isn't for the other person? Anger and resentment are poisons in our body. The tighter we hold onto them, the sicker we become. Each per- son has the right to live out their own life, the freedom to live as they please. For us to take that away from them is to steal away their rights as a human. Many will not follow the path we take. Some may even try, but will fall short. It is up to us to work on our own path, to lead the way for ourselves.

Resenting another because they have chosen to live in a way that is not aligned with our own, only poisons us. To find forgiveness in the midst of our pain is to know true freedom. Forgive, let go, be free. No one needs to change in order for you to be happy. Only you can do that for yourself.

Ask Yourself: What If Forgiveness Isn't for the Other Person?

_____

_____

_____

_____

_____

_____

_____

_____

CHAPTER SIXTY-THREE

What If You Fell in Love with Life Exactly How it is?

Being in love can be a wonderful experience. When we're in love, we will do just about anything. Drive for hours, change our diet, the list goes on. All we want is to be around what we are in love with. Imagine if you were in love with life. What would you do? How would you act? What lengths would you go to in order to make life happy?

When you fall in love with life, it will love you back. Imagine being in a relationship with an unlimited amount of joy, love, compassion, and happiness. With more excitement than you know what to do with. That is a relationship with life. Of course you have to bring something to that table as well: Your love.

Ask Yourself: What If You Fell in Love with Life Exactly How it is?

_____

_____

_____

_____

_____

_____

_____

CHAPTER SIXTY-FOUR

What If You Embrace Change Instead of Fighting It?

Change, the only constant thing we have. Yet millions of people fight against it with all they have. They live in fear of it, pushing back against whatever it brings. Even ruining their chances at a more fulfilling life because of it. What if you embrace change in- stead of fighting it? If you can hold change as you would a dear friend, you could see a tremendous growth pattern in your life.

I used to run from change, always hoping I could stay in my comfort zone, or at least get back to it. Then when an aware- ness occurred, everything changed. I know now that to fully live, to experience true joy, to know real freedom is, I must not only embrace change but welcome it in. Each day I step into the unknown. Each day I welcome change to occur. Holding a vision of the joy, passion, and freedom I want to experience while allowing the unknown to unfold it for me. It is in the unknown that magic happens. It is through change that all possibilities can manifest. Allow, surrender, and move with the change.

Ask Yourself: What If You Embrace Change Instead of Fighting It?

_____

_____

_____

_____

_____

_____

_____

CHAPTER SIXTY-FIVE

What If You Replaced Your Anger With Compassion?

We can't be angry at our anger. It did its job. We used it to survive. With the awareness that we no longer need anger, comes a void we must fill. If we no longer want to base our decisions on anger, if we no longer want to feel our anger and allow angry thoughts to control us, we must release it.

Getting rid of your anger is the first step. What comes next is what to replace it with? I have found that when my survival instincts manufacture anger, my best solution is to replace it with compassion. When I'm angry, I pause, reflect on my attachment, then decide to replace it with compassion. Compassion for myself, for being human and having survival emotions. And compassion for the external circumstance, person, place, or thing that I feel has caused my anger. They do not know what they have done and in that moment, I can forgive the human in them as well as myself.

Ask Yourself: What If You Replaced Your Anger With Compassion?

_____

_____

_____

_____

_____

_____

CHAPTER SIXTY-SIX

What If Everyone Approved of Every Decision You Wanted to Make?

All too often, our decisions are based on the opinions of others. We instantly wonder, what will my parents think? What will my spouse think? How would my friends react if I did that? What if everyone approved of your decisions? What would you do if the whole world agreed with your next choice?

The reality is, most people deflect this possibility simply because of one word: Responsibility. You see, if everyone approved of every decision, then your life would be entirely up to you. No one to blame, nothing to fall back on, just you. Can you accept that level of responsibility? To own your life fully?

In truth, those who love you will support you no matter what you choose and no matter what decision you make. Those who judge you were going to judge you no matter what you did otherwise. Accept responsibility for what it is you truly want and own all that comes with it. This one life is too short to be wasted on the opinions of others. Approve of yourself, decide, then act.

Ask Yourself: What If Everyone Approved of Every Decision You Wanted to Make?

_____

_____

_____

_____

_____

_____

CHAPTER SIXTY-SEVEN

What If the Direction of the World Was Decided By Your Next Decision?

Sometimes we feel small. We feel insignificant in the grand scheme of things. What if the direction of the world was decided by your next decision? Many people feel as if their voice is never heard, by those closest to them as well as the world itself. With seven and a half billion people, it's easy to get lost in the crowd. All it takes is one person to change its course forever.

Just think for a moment about what it would be like to have your next choice dictate the trajectory of our planet. How would you act? How much thought would you put into it? How would you feel about your next choice? Take it in for a moment. That is how you should make every decision in your life. You are the world. Your life is as important as this entire planet. Your next choice could alter human history, but if nothing else, it will alter your history.

Ask Yourself: What If the Direction of the World Was Decided By Your Next Decision?

_____

_____

_____

_____

_____

_____

_____

CHAPTER SIXTY-EIGHT

What If Life Had More to Offer than You Could Imagine for Yourself?

When asked the question, "What do you really want?" Half of everyone will shout out things they think will make them happy, the other half don't even know where to start. Even if we could decide right now to have every item on our list, wouldn't that only be the capacity at which we can envision in this moment? Do we honestly believe that who we are today knows what the version of us five years from now will want?

Even if we could create it now, wouldn't we be limiting ourselves from what our current imagination can conjure up? Knowing that our current ideas are at best the highest versions of what our past self can think of, I wonder if maybe life itself has more to offer. What if life had more in store for us than we can even imagine for ourselves? Let go. Die each moment, so you can be born free in the next.

Ask Yourself: What If Life Had More to Offer than You Could Imagine for Yourself?

_____

_____

_____

_____

_____

_____

_____

FINAL THOUGHTS

I want you to reward yourself by giving yourself time to digest what you've read in these pages. Not many people will pick up a book like this to read let alone finish reading it. Many of the concepts left here with you and have the ability to completely shift the way you perceive the world and the intention is to free you of the ties that bind you into staying stuck. Take what you want and leave the rest. In the end it must be a decision you make to unravel each thought and concept into what works best for you. For more information on how to create the life you want both internally and externally you can reach out to Corey Gladwell at CoreyGladwell.com. You'll find coaching, programs he offers and tons of free trainings to dive into as well as his other books. You can also book him to speak at your next event. We must make up our own minds to live the life we want. You have the power within you to do just that. After all it is the depth of our consciousness that will determine our capacity for experience.

PERSONAL NOTES

PERSONAL NOTES

PERSONAL NOTES

PERSONAL NOTES

PERSONAL NOTES

PERSONAL NOTES

Personal notes

PERSONAL NOTES